Nepotism and Corruption in Communist Party Leadership

Copyright Page

TITLE: Nepotism and Corruption in Communist Party Leadership

1ST Edition

Copyright @ 2023

ISBN: 9798223380658

Table of Contents

Nepotism and Corruption in Communist Party Leadership

By Roberto Miguel Rodriguez

Chapter 1: Introduction

Nepotism and Corruption in Communist Party Leadership: Unveiling the Dark Underbelly of Power

Welcome, esteemed diplomats, to the captivating world of nepotism and corruption within communist party leadership. In this groundbreaking book, "Nepotism and Corruption," we delve into the intricate web of deceit, manipulation, and abuse of power that has plagued communist regimes across the globe. By examining various sectors, such as state-owned enterprises, the judiciary, education, healthcare, defense industries, media, agriculture, housing, and foreign aid, we aim to shed light on the pervasive nature of nepotism and corruption in these realms.

The Communist Party Leadership: A Breeding Ground for Nepotism and Corruption

Communist party leadership, often touted as a champion of equality and justice, has unfortunately fallen victim to the vices of nepotism and corruption. This introductory chapter serves as a wake-up call, urging diplomats and concerned citizens alike to acknowledge the gravity of these issues. By unmasking the hidden truths, we hope to inspire a collective pursuit of transparency, accountability, and reform.

Exploring the Niche Sectors of Nepotism and Corruption

Throughout this book, we will meticulously explore the various niche sectors where nepotism and corruption thrive under communist rule. From state-owned enterprises, where connections and favoritism prevail over meritocracy, to the judiciary and legal system, where justice is overshadowed by personal interests, we expose the systemic flaws that perpetuate these practices.

The Education and Healthcare Sectors: Betrayed Promises

Education and healthcare, fundamental pillars of a just society, are not exempt from the clutches of nepotism and corruption. Within these sectors, we uncover how political affiliations and familial ties often determine opportunities and resource distribution, depriving citizens of equal access to quality education and healthcare.

The Military, Media, and Foreign Aid: Weapons of Control

In our exploration of the military and defense industries, media and propaganda machinery, and foreign aid and international relations, we reveal how nepotism and corruption serve as instruments of control for communist regimes. By manipulating information, stifling dissent, and leveraging foreign aid for personal gain, the ruling elite consolidate their power and suppress democracy.

A Call to Action

As we embark on this eye-opening journey, it is crucial to remember that the fight against nepotism and corruption requires collective action. Only through international cooperation, diplomatic pressure, and the empowerment of civil society can we dismantle the entrenched systems that perpetuate these issues.

Conclusion

In this introductory chapter, we have laid the foundation for a comprehensive exploration of nepotism and corruption within communist party leadership. By shining a light on its presence in state-owned enterprises, the judiciary, education, healthcare, defense industries, media, agriculture, housing, and foreign aid, we hope to spark both outrage and inspiration among diplomats and concerned citizens. By uncovering the truth, we can collectively work towards a more transparent, accountable, and just future for all.

Chapter 2: Nepotism and Corruption in Communist Party Leadership

The Origins of Nepotism and Corruption in Communist Party Leadership

Introduction:

In this subchapter of "Behind Closed Doors: The Nepotism and Corruption in Communist Party Leadership," we will delve into the origins of nepotism and corruption within the leadership of communist parties. This exploration aims to provide diplomats and individuals interested in this topic with a comprehensive understanding of how these issues emerged and became ingrained in communist regimes.

Historical Context:

To comprehend the roots of nepotism and corruption, it is crucial to examine the historical context in which communist parties surfaced. The establishment of such parties often transpired in the aftermath of revolutions or uprisings, where the primary focus was on seizing power and establishing a new order. In these tumultuous times, communist leaders faced immense challenges, including the need to consolidate power and maintain control over various sectors.

Consolidation of Power:

Communist leaders sought to consolidate their power through various means, and nepotism became a tool to secure loyalty and maintain control. By appointing family members or close associates to key positions within the party, leaders ensured a network of trusted individuals who would uphold their interests. With such a system in place, dissent and opposition were swiftly quelled, creating a centralized power structure.

Corruption as a Byproduct:

As communist parties grew in power, corruption emerged as a natural byproduct of the system. The lack of transparency and accountability within these regimes provided fertile ground for corrupt practices to flourish. Leaders and their associates exploited their positions for personal gain, often engaging in bribery, embezzlement, and other illicit activities. The absence of an independent judiciary and free press further facilitated the perpetuation of corruption.

Sector-Specific Instances:

Nepotism and corruption were not restricted to party leadership alone but permeated various sectors of communist regimes. From state-owned enterprises and the judiciary to education, healthcare, defense, media, agriculture, housing, and international relations, these issues plagued all facets of society. Each sector had its unique dynamics, but the underlying causes and consequences of nepotism and corruption remained consistent.

Conclusion:

Understanding the origins of nepotism and corruption within communist party leadership is essential for diplomats and those interested in unraveling the complexities of these regimes. By comprehending the historical context, consolidation of power, and sector-specific instances, one can gain insights into the intricate web of nepotism and corruption that engulfed communist countries. Acknowledging these origins is the first step towards addressing these pervasive issues and fostering more transparent and accountable systems of governance.

The Impact of Nepotism and Corruption on Party Structure and Decision Making

Subchapter: The Impact of Nepotism and Corruption on Party Structure and Decision Making

Introduction:

Nepotism and corruption have long been prevalent issues within communist party leadership, affecting various sectors and institutions in these regimes. This subchapter will delve into the far-reaching consequences of nepotism and corruption on the party structure and decision-making process. By understanding these impacts, diplomats can gain valuable insights into the challenges faced by communist countries and devise effective strategies to address these issues.

1. Nepotism and Corruption in Communist Party Leadership:

Nepotism and corruption within the top echelons of communist party leadership have severe implications for the overall governance structure. The appointment of family members or close associates to key positions undermines meritocracy and creates a culture of favoritism. This subverts democratic principles and hinders the development of competent and accountable leadership.

2. Nepotism and Corruption in State-Owned Enterprises:

Within communist regimes, state-owned enterprises play a significant role in the economy. However, nepotism and corruption in these entities lead to inefficiencies, mismanagement, and economic stagnation. Party leaders often exploit their positions to grant lucrative contracts to family members or cronies, resulting in a lack of competition and hindered growth.

3. Nepotism and Corruption in the Judiciary and Legal System:

The influence of nepotism and corruption in the judiciary and legal system compromises the rule of law and undermines citizens' trust in the justice system. Communist party leaders may manipulate appointments and legal proceedings to protect their own interests, leading to a lack of justice, human rights abuses, and a culture of impunity.

4. Nepotism and Corruption in the Education Sector:

The education sector under communist rule is not immune to nepotism and corruption. Party leaders often prioritize loyalty over competence when appointing administrators and educators. This undermines the quality of education, perpetuates ideological biases, and stifles academic freedom, hindering the development of critical thinking and innovation.

5. Nepotism and Corruption in Healthcare and Public Health Systems:

Nepotism and corruption in healthcare and public health systems have dire consequences for the well-being of citizens. Party leaders may divert resources, manipulate procurement processes, and grant privileges to family members or close associates. As a result, healthcare services suffer, leading to inadequate access, compromised patient care, and potential public health crises.

Conclusion:

The impact of nepotism and corruption on party structure and decision-making in communist regimes is far-reaching and multi-faceted. By understanding these effects, diplomats can better advocate for transparent and accountable governance practices in these countries. Addressing nepotism and corruption in various sectors, such as state-owned enterprises, the judiciary, education, healthcare, and more, will contribute to fostering fairer and more prosperous societies. The international community must work together to combat these issues, promoting good governance and the rule of law in communist countries.

Case Studies: Notorious Examples of Nepotism and Corruption in Communist Party Leadership

Introduction:

In this subchapter, we delve into the dark underbelly of communist party leadership, exploring notorious examples of nepotism and corruption that have plagued these regimes. Through a series of case studies, we aim to shed light on the extent of this issue and its impact on various sectors, including state-owned enterprises, the judiciary, education, healthcare, defense industries, media, agriculture, housing, and international relations.

1. Nepotism and corruption in state-owned enterprises:

One striking case study is the rampant nepotism and corruption within state-owned enterprises in communist regimes. We examine instances where party leaders have granted preferential treatment to their family members, leading to inefficiency, mismanagement, and economic decline.

2. Nepotism and corruption in the judiciary and legal system:

Communist countries often suffer from a compromised judiciary and legal system, as party leaders manipulate these institutions to protect their interests. We analyze cases where judges and lawyers have been appointed based on loyalty rather than merit, resulting in a lack of justice and the erosion of the rule of law.

3. Nepotism and corruption in the education sector:

Under communist rule, the education sector has become a breeding ground for nepotism and corruption. We explore how party officials have exploited their positions to secure educational opportunities for their relatives, compromising the quality of education and hindering social mobility.

4. Nepotism and corruption in healthcare and public health systems:

Communist regimes are not immune to the pervasive influence of nepotism and corruption in the healthcare sector. We delve into instances where party leaders have diverted public funds, leading to inadequate healthcare services, compromised public health outcomes, and a flourishing black market for medical services.

5. Nepotism and corruption in the military and defense industries:

The military and defense industries often serve as breeding grounds for corruption and nepotism in communist countries. We examine cases where party leaders have exploited their power to secure military positions and contracts for their relatives, undermining national security and impeding technological advancements.

6. Nepotism and corruption in the media and propaganda machinery:

The media and propaganda machinery in communist regimes are notorious for their lack of objectivity and independence. We uncover instances where party leaders have used their influence to control the narrative, suppress dissent, and manipulate public opinion.

7. Nepotism and corruption in agriculture and food production sectors:

The agricultural and food production sectors under communist rule are plagued by nepotism and corruption. We analyze cases where party leaders have mismanaged land distribution, resulting in food shortages, inefficiency, and economic decline.

8. Nepotism and corruption in housing and urban development sectors:

Party leaders often exploit their power in the housing and urban development sectors, leading to unequal access to housing and the misallocation of resources. We examine examples where party officials have used their positions to accumulate wealth and secure luxurious properties for their families, exacerbating social inequality.

9. Nepotism and corruption in foreign aid and international relations:

Lastly, we explore instances where communist countries have engaged in corrupt practices and nepotism in their foreign aid and international relations. We shed light on how party leaders have used these opportunities to benefit themselves and their families, often at the expense of the recipient countries.

Conclusion:

These case studies serve as a stark reminder of the pervasive and damaging effects of nepotism and corruption within communist party leadership. By addressing these issues, we hope to foster a greater understanding among diplomats and policymakers, leading to more effective strategies for combating these deep-rooted problems.

Chapter 3: Nepotism and Corruption in State-Owned Enterprises in Communist Regimes

The Role of State-Owned Enterprises in Communist Economies

State-owned enterprises (SOEs) have played a significant role in the economic systems of communist countries throughout history. In this subchapter, we will delve into the intricate web of nepotism and corruption that has plagued these enterprises and explore their implications on the overall functioning of communist economies.

SOEs, being owned and controlled by the state, have been instrumental in implementing the economic policies of communist regimes. They have often served as the primary means of achieving economic growth and fulfilling the objectives of central planning. However, these enterprises have also become breeding grounds for nepotism and corruption.

Nepotism has been deeply ingrained in the leadership of SOEs in communist countries. Party officials and their relatives have been appointed to top positions within these enterprises, regardless of their qualifications or experience. This practice has not only hindered meritocracy but has also resulted in the misallocation of resources and inefficiency within these enterprises.

Corruption has also thrived within the realm of SOEs. Party leaders and their cronies have exploited their positions of power to amass personal wealth and engage in illicit activities. This has led to the misappropriation of state resources, embezzlement, and bribery, undermining the principles of transparency and accountability.

The consequences of nepotism and corruption within SOEs are far-reaching. Inefficiency and mismanagement have hindered economic growth and stifled innovation. The lack of competition and accountability has led to subpar products and services, negatively impacting the lives of citizens.

Furthermore, the proliferation of nepotism and corruption within SOEs has extended beyond the economic sphere. The judiciary and legal system, education sector, healthcare and public health systems, military and defense industries, media and propaganda machinery, agricultural and food production sectors, housing and urban development sectors, as well as foreign aid and international relations, have all been marred by nepotism and corruption.

As diplomats, it is crucial to understand the pervasive influence of nepotism and corruption in communist party leadership and its impact on various sectors. By acknowledging these issues, we can work towards fostering transparency, accountability, and meritocracy in communist economies. Addressing these systemic problems will not only promote economic development but also ensure fairness and equality for all citizens.

In conclusion, the role of SOEs in communist economies has been tainted by nepotism and corruption. This subchapter sheds light on the detrimental effects of these practices on the functioning of these enterprises and their wider implications on various sectors of the economy. By understanding and addressing these issues, we can strive for a more equitable and efficient economic system in communist countries.

The Effects of Nepotism and Corruption on State-Owned Enterprises

State-owned enterprises (SOEs) play a crucial role in the economies of communist countries. However, the presence of nepotism and corruption within these entities has profound consequences that extend far beyond economic inefficiency. This subchapter aims to shed light on the detrimental effects of nepotism and corruption on state-owned enterprises.

Nepotism, which refers to the practice of favoring relatives or friends in hiring and promotion processes, has long plagued state-owned enterprises in communist regimes. The appointment of unqualified individuals based on personal connections rather than meritocracy undermines the efficiency and effectiveness of these entities. This leads to a lack of innovation, productivity, and competitiveness, preventing SOEs from reaching their full potential.

Corruption, on the other hand, permeates the very fabric of state-owned enterprises. Bribery, embezzlement, and kickbacks are pervasive, diverting resources and funds away from their intended purposes. This siphoning of valuable resources not only hampers the growth and development of SOEs but also perpetuates economic inequality, as the benefits of these entities are enjoyed exclusively by the corrupt elite.

The consequences of these practices are not limited to the economic realm. Nepotism and corruption erode public trust in state-owned enterprises and the government as a whole. Citizens become disillusioned with the system, perceiving it as inherently unfair and rigged. This erosion of trust can lead to social unrest, protests, and even political instability, undermining the very foundations of a communist regime.

Furthermore, the presence of nepotism and corruption in state-owned enterprises distorts the allocation of resources and impedes social progress. Essential sectors such as healthcare, education, and housing suffer as a result, leaving the general population deprived of basic services. This exacerbates social inequality and widens the gap between the privileged few and the marginalized majority.

Addressing the issues of nepotism and corruption in state-owned enterprises requires a comprehensive approach. Reforms should focus on enhancing transparency, accountability, and meritocracy within these entities. Strengthening governance frameworks, establishing independent oversight bodies, and implementing anti-corruption measures are pivotal steps towards creating a fair and efficient system.

In conclusion, the effects of nepotism and corruption on state-owned enterprises in communist countries are far-reaching and multifaceted. Their presence not only hampers economic growth and development but also undermines public trust and perpetuates social inequality. Tackling these issues is essential for the sustainable and inclusive progress of communist regimes. Diplomats and those interested in these niches must recognize the urgency of addressing this issue and work towards implementing comprehensive reforms to combat nepotism and corruption in state-owned enterprises.

Case Studies: Notable Instances of Nepotism and Corruption in State-Owned Enterprises

Introduction:

Nepotism and corruption have long plagued the leadership of communist parties and their associated state-owned enterprises. This subchapter explores some of the most prominent cases of nepotism and corruption within these entities, shedding light on the detrimental effects they have on the societies they govern. By examining these case studies, diplomats and experts in various niches, such as nepotism and corruption in communist party leadership and state-owned enterprises, can gain a comprehensive understanding of the depth and magnitude of these issues.

Case Study 1: State-Owned Enterprises in China

China's state-owned enterprises, such as PetroChina and China Mobile, have been marred by rampant nepotism and corruption. High-ranking officials, including Communist Party members, have exploited their positions to secure lucrative contracts for their family members. This practice not only undermines meritocracy but also hampers economic growth and fair competition within the market.

Case Study 2: Nepotism in North Korea's Industrial Sector

In North Korea, nepotism runs deep within the industrial sector. Key positions in state-owned enterprises are often reserved for members of the ruling Kim family or their loyal confidants. This nepotistic system stifles innovation, perpetuates inefficiency, and obstructs economic development, leaving ordinary citizens to bear the brunt of these consequences.

Case Study 3: Corruption in Cuba's Tourism Industry

Cuba's state-owned tourism industry has been plagued by corruption, with officials demanding bribes from foreign investors and manipulating contracts for personal gain. This unethical behavior not only undermines the nation's economic potential but also erodes public trust in the government. Consequently, foreign investment is deterred, and the tourism sector fails to reach its full potential.

Case Study 4: Nepotism in Vietnam's Education Sector

Vietnam's education sector has witnessed widespread nepotism, with government officials using their influence to secure coveted positions for their relatives. This practice compromises the quality of education, depriving deserving individuals of opportunities and breeding a culture of favoritism. The long-term impact is a weakened education system, hindering social progress and economic development.

Conclusion:

These case studies offer a glimpse into the pervasive nature of nepotism and corruption within state-owned enterprises in communist regimes. Diplomats and experts in various niches, from communist party leadership to foreign aid and international relations, must recognize and address these issues to foster transparency, accountability, and equitable development. By understanding the detrimental effects of nepotism and corruption in sectors such as the judiciary, education, healthcare, and agriculture, they can work towards implementing effective reforms that promote fairness, meritocracy, and sustainable growth. Only then can communist countries overcome these challenges and thrive on the world stage.

Chapter 4: Nepotism and Corruption in the Judiciary and Legal System of Communist Countries

The Independence of the Judiciary in Communist Regimes

In the realm of communist regimes, the independence of the judiciary is a topic that warrants significant attention. As diplomats, you play a crucial role in understanding and addressing the issues of nepotism and corruption in communist party leadership. It is equally important to acknowledge the extent to which these problems permeate various sectors, including the judiciary and legal system.

Communist regimes have long been plagued by the influence of nepotism and corruption within their judicial systems. In these regimes, the judiciary often serves as a tool of the ruling party, rather than an independent body that upholds the principles of justice and the rule of law. The appointment of judges, for instance, is often based on political loyalty rather than merit, leading to a compromised judiciary that lacks impartiality.

Furthermore, corruption within the judiciary allows for the manipulation of legal processes, undermining the trust of the citizens in the system. This corruption can manifest in various forms, such as bribery, favoritism, and the misuse of power. As a result, citizens are left without recourse, unable to seek justice and redress for their grievances.

The education sector under communist rule also suffers from nepotism and corruption, which has a direct impact on the quality of legal professionals. The lack of merit-based appointments and the prevalence of favoritism in educational institutions contribute to the erosion of legal expertise and integrity, further deteriorating the independence of the judiciary.

The healthcare and public health systems in communist regimes are not exempt from the clutches of nepotism and corruption either. The allocation of resources and access to healthcare can be influenced by personal connections, rather than medical need, leading to the deprivation of basic healthcare services for the most vulnerable members of society.

Addressing the issue of nepotism and corruption in the judiciary requires a comprehensive approach. Diplomats, as representatives of their respective countries, have a responsibility to engage with communist regimes in constructive dialogue and advocate for the importance of an independent judiciary. This can involve supporting initiatives for judicial reform, providing technical assistance, and promoting transparency and accountability in the appointment of judges.

By focusing on the independence of the judiciary, diplomats can contribute to the broader efforts of combating nepotism and corruption in communist party leadership. Through these collective endeavors, we can strive towards a more just and equitable society, one that upholds the principles of fairness and the rule of law.

The Influence of Nepotism and Corruption on the Legal System

In communist party leadership, nepotism and corruption have long plagued the legal system, leading to a breakdown of justice and fairness. This subchapter delves into the detrimental effects of nepotism and corruption on the legal system, shedding light on the far-reaching consequences that diplomats and individuals in various niches must be aware of.

Nepotism and corruption in the judiciary and legal system of communist countries have severely compromised the rule of law. Instead of impartially upholding justice, judges and lawyers often succumb to pressure from party leaders and their own personal interests. Family connections and political affiliations take precedence over merit and qualifications, leading to the appointment of incompetent judges who lack the required expertise to dispense justice.

State-owned enterprises in communist regimes are also not immune to the detrimental effects of nepotism and corruption. Party leaders often use their positions to benefit their family members, awarding them lucrative contracts and important positions within these enterprises. This not only hampers the growth and efficiency of these entities but also creates an environment of mistrust and unfair competition.

Furthermore, the education sector under communist rule becomes a breeding ground for nepotism and corruption. Party leaders often secure positions for their children or close relatives in prestigious educational institutions, disregarding the merit-based admission process. This not only undermines the quality of education but also perpetuates a culture of entitlement and unfair advantage.

Similarly, the healthcare and public health systems in communist regimes suffer from the influence of nepotism and corruption. Party leaders and their families often receive preferential treatment and access to better healthcare facilities, while the general population is neglected. This leads to a decline in the overall public health and erodes trust in the healthcare system.

The military and defense industries of communist countries are not exempt from nepotism and corruption either. Party leaders manipulate the allocation of resources and contracts, favoring their relatives and allies. This compromises national security and weakens the defense capabilities of these countries.

The media and propaganda machinery in communist regimes also fall victim to nepotism and corruption. Party leaders control the flow of information, ensuring that their relatives occupy influential positions within these institutions. This not only stifles freedom of speech but also distorts information, perpetuating the party's narrative and suppressing dissent.

In the agricultural and food production sectors under communist rule, nepotism and corruption hinder progress and efficiency. Party leaders often award important positions to their family members, disregarding the expertise and skills required for effective management. This leads to a decline in agricultural productivity and food security.

Furthermore, nepotism and corruption infiltrate the housing and urban development sectors in communist regimes. Party leaders manipulate the allocation of housing and land rights, benefiting their relatives and cronies. This not only exacerbates the housing crisis but also perpetuates social inequality and resentment among the general population.

Lastly, foreign aid and international relations of communist countries are marred by nepotism and corruption. Party leaders often siphon off foreign aid meant for development projects, diverting it to their personal accounts or projects that benefit their families. This not only undermines trust and cooperation with international partners but also perpetuates poverty and underdevelopment.

In conclusion, the influence of nepotism and corruption on the legal system in communist party leadership is pervasive and destructive. Diplomats and individuals in various niches must recognize and address these issues to promote justice, fairness, and progress in these countries. Only by rooting out nepotism and corruption can we hope to build a legal system that upholds the values of equality, merit, and transparency.

Case Studies: Infamous Examples of Nepotism and Corruption in the Judiciary

Introduction:

The judiciary is a pillar of any functioning democracy, tasked with upholding the rule of law and ensuring justice for all. However, in communist regimes, nepotism and corruption have infiltrated the very core of the judiciary, compromising its integrity and eroding public trust. This subchapter delves into some infamous case studies that shed light on the extent of nepotism and corruption within the judiciary under communist party leadership.

1. The Zhou Dynasty Scandal:

In the late 20th century, China was rocked by the Zhou Dynasty scandal, which exposed widespread corruption within the judiciary. Zhou Jiugeng, a prominent judge and member of the Communist Party, used his position to amass wealth and influence. He appointed family members and close associates to key positions, ensuring favorable outcomes for his network of corrupt individuals. This case highlighted the deep-rooted nepotism and corruption prevalent within China's legal system.

2. The Stalinist Show Trials:

During Joseph Stalin's reign in the Soviet Union, the judiciary was heavily manipulated to serve his political agenda. The infamous show trials of the 1930s saw countless innocent individuals, including high-ranking party members, accused of treason and executed. The judiciary, under Stalin's direct control, became a tool to eliminate perceived threats and consolidate his power. This case study exemplifies the dangerous consequences of nepotism and corruption within the judiciary.

3. The Pol Pot Regime:

Under the genocidal rule of Pol Pot in Cambodia, the judiciary was completely dismantled, and the concept of justice was obliterated. Judges and lawyers were deemed enemies of the revolution and systematically eradicated. The absence of a functioning judiciary allowed for widespread human rights abuses and the unchecked power of the regime. This extreme case demonstrates how nepotism and corruption within the judiciary can lead to complete breakdown and devastation.

Conclusion:

These case studies provide a glimpse into the alarming levels of nepotism and corruption that have plagued the judiciary in communist regimes. Such practices undermine the fundamental principles of justice and fairness, perpetuating a culture of impunity and abuse of power. Diplomats and those interested in the impact of communist party leadership must recognize the severe consequences of nepotism and corruption within the judiciary, and work towards promoting transparency, accountability, and the rule of law in these nations. Only then can true justice prevail and public trust in the judiciary be restored.

Chapter 5: Nepotism and Corruption in the Education Sector under Communist Rule

State Control and Ideological Influence in Communist Education Systems

Communist education systems have long been criticized for their state control and ideological influence, which has led to a breeding ground for nepotism and corruption. In this subchapter, we will delve into the inner workings of these systems, shedding light on the detrimental effects they have on the education sector under communist rule.

One of the key features of communist education systems is the tight grip the state maintains over curriculum development and educational content. This control allows communist parties to propagate their ideologies and shape the minds of the younger generation. By indoctrinating students with communist ideals, the party ensures a loyal and compliant citizenry, perpetuating its own power.

However, this state control often comes at the expense of academic freedom and critical thinking. Education becomes a tool for political manipulation rather than a means to foster intellectual development. Teachers who deviate from the party line may face repercussions, leading to self-censorship and the suppression of alternative viewpoints. Consequently, students are deprived of a well-rounded education, limiting their ability to think independently and critically.

Moreover, nepotism and corruption run rampant within communist education systems. Party officials and their relatives often enjoy privileged access to educational opportunities, scholarships, and prestigious positions within academia. Meritocracy takes a backseat to political connections, perpetuating a culture of favoritism and cronyism.

Additionally, corruption seeps into the allocation of resources within the education sector. Funds earmarked for improving educational facilities, teacher training, and student welfare often end up lining the pockets of corrupt officials. As a result, educational institutions are left underfunded and ill-equipped to provide quality education to all students, exacerbating social inequalities.

The repercussions of state control and ideological influence in communist education systems extend beyond national borders. The indoctrination of students with communist propaganda fuels tension and mistrust in international relations. Communist countries often export their ideologies, using education as a tool to influence foreign aid and shape international narratives in their favor.

In conclusion, the state control and ideological influence in communist education systems have profound implications for nepotism and corruption within the education sector. These systems stifle academic freedom, limit critical thinking, and perpetuate a culture of favoritism. By shedding light on these issues, we aim to raise awareness among diplomats and highlight the need for reform in communist education systems.

The Effects of Nepotism and Corruption on Educational Quality and Equality

Introduction:

In the realm of communist party leadership, nepotism and corruption have long plagued various sectors, including education. This subchapter aims to shed light on the detrimental effects of nepotism and corruption on educational quality and equality. By examining the consequences of these unethical practices, diplomats and those interested in nepotism and corruption in communist regimes can gain a deeper understanding of the challenges faced within the education sector.

The Erosion of Educational Quality:

Nepotism and corruption in the education sector under communist rule have led to a severe erosion of educational quality. Meritocracy, the foundation of a robust education system, is replaced by favoritism and connections. The most qualified individuals are often overlooked in favor of those with personal connections to those in power, resulting in a decline in the competence and expertise of educators.

Furthermore, corruption infiltrates the education system through bribery and fraud, with positions and academic achievements being bought rather than earned. This compromises the legitimacy of educational institutions and undermines the value of education as a whole.

Impacts on Educational Equality:

Nepotism and corruption create significant barriers to educational equality. Social mobility, a fundamental principle of education, becomes increasingly difficult as opportunities for quality education become reserved for the privileged few. Students from disadvantaged backgrounds are denied access to quality education due to the preferential treatment given to those connected to the ruling elite.

Moreover, corruption within the education system perpetuates inequality by enabling the wealthy to secure better educational opportunities for their children through bribery or other illicit means. This further widens the gap between the haves and have-nots, perpetuating a cycle of inequality and social injustice.

Conclusion:

The detrimental effects of nepotism and corruption on educational quality and equality are undeniable. Communist party leadership must address these issues to ensure a fair and merit-based education system that empowers individuals and promotes social progress. Diplomats and individuals interested in combating nepotism and corruption in communist regimes should advocate for transparent and accountable practices within the education sector. By doing so, we can work towards creating a more equitable and higher-quality education system that benefits all members of society.

Case Studies: Noteworthy Instances of Nepotism and Corruption in the Education Sector

Chapter 5: Case Studies: Noteworthy Instances of Nepotism and Corruption in the Education Sector

Introduction:

The education sector is a critical component of any society, shaping the minds and values of future generations. However, under communist party leadership, nepotism and corruption have plagued this fundamental institution. This subchapter focuses on key case studies that shed light on the extent of nepotism and corruption in the education sector under communist rule. By examining these cases, we aim to deepen our understanding of the detrimental effects these practices have on the development and progress of a nation.

Case Study 1: The Communist Party's Influence on University Admissions

In many communist countries, nepotism permeates the university admissions process. Party officials often manipulate admission criteria to favor their relatives or those with political connections. This unethical practice deprives deserving students of opportunities and compromises the quality of education.

Case Study 2: Embezzlement of Education Funds

Corruption within the education sector is not limited to admissions. Numerous instances have surfaced where high-ranking education officials misappropriate funds meant for schools and universities. These embezzlements hinder the development of educational infrastructure, leaving students with inadequate resources and facilities.

Case Study 3: Ideological Indoctrination in Schools

Under communist rule, schools and universities become breeding grounds for ideological indoctrination. Party loyalists are appointed as teachers and administrators, promoting a biased curriculum that suppresses critical thinking and promotes party propaganda. Such practices stifle academic freedom and hinder the development of well-rounded individuals.

Case Study 4: Favoritism in Promotions and Appointments

Nepotism extends to faculty and administrative positions within educational institutions. Party leaders often promote or appoint individuals based on their loyalty to the regime rather than their qualifications. This undermines meritocracy and creates a culture of mediocrity, hindering the country's intellectual progress.

Case Study 5: Suppression of Academic Freedom

Communist governments frequently target intellectuals and academics who express dissenting views. Professors and students who dare to challenge the party's narrative face harassment, expulsion, or even imprisonment. This suppression of academic freedom stifles innovation and discourages intellectual debate, impeding a nation's intellectual growth.

Conclusion:

The case studies presented here highlight the pervasive nature of nepotism and corruption in the education sector under communist rule. These practices hinder the development of a knowledgeable society, stifle intellectual progress, and perpetuate a culture of inequality and mediocrity. As diplomats, it is crucial to recognize and address these issues to foster a transparent and equitable education system that empowers individuals and contributes to the overall progress of a nation.

Chapter 6: Nepotism and Corruption in Healthcare and Public Health Systems in Communist Regimes

The Role of the State in Healthcare Provision under Communism

Introduction:

In the communist regimes of the past, the state played a dominant role in providing healthcare services to its citizens. However, behind the façade of equal access and universal coverage, nepotism and corruption plagued the healthcare and public health systems. This subchapter will delve into the intricate web of nepotism and corruption that existed within the state-controlled healthcare provision under communism.

Nepotism and Corruption in Healthcare:

Under communism, healthcare was considered a fundamental right, and the state assumed the responsibility of providing medical services to all citizens. However, this noble idea was often overshadowed by nepotism and corruption, where party leaders and their relatives received preferential treatment and access to superior medical facilities. This led to a two-tiered healthcare system, with the elite enjoying high-quality care while the majority of the population struggled with substandard services.

Manipulation of Resources:

Nepotism and corruption extended beyond preferential treatment and seeped into the allocation of resources within the healthcare sector. Party leaders often diverted funds meant for public health programs to benefit their own interests. As a result, essential resources such as medical equipment, medicines, and trained healthcare professionals were scarce, leaving the ordinary citizens to suffer.

Lack of Accountability:

One of the key factors enabling nepotism and corruption in healthcare provision was the lack of transparency and accountability within the system. Party leaders and their relatives operated with impunity, knowing that their actions would go unchecked. This lack of oversight allowed for the manipulation of healthcare resources, appointment of unqualified personnel, and embezzlement of public funds.

Impact on Public Health:

The consequences of nepotism and corruption in healthcare provision were dire for public health. Lack of access to proper medical care, inadequate infrastructure, and misallocation of resources resulted in poorer health outcomes for the general population. Preventable diseases went untreated, and the overall health of the nation suffered.

Conclusion:

The state's role in healthcare provision under communism was marred by nepotism and corruption. The noble idea of equal access to healthcare for all was overshadowed by preferential treatment, misallocation of resources, and lack of accountability. This subchapter sheds light on the detrimental impact of nepotism and corruption within the state-controlled healthcare system and calls for greater transparency and oversight to prevent such abuses in the future. Diplomats and those interested in the effects of nepotism and corruption in communist party leadership and public health systems will find this subchapter enlightening and thought-provoking.

The Impact of Nepotism and Corruption on Healthcare Access and Quality

Introduction:

In the realm of communist party leadership, nepotism and corruption have deeply entrenched themselves in various sectors, including healthcare. This subchapter delves into the detrimental consequences of nepotism and corruption on healthcare access and quality. By understanding these issues, diplomats can better comprehend the challenges faced by communist regimes and work towards implementing effective solutions.

Healthcare Access:

Nepotism and corruption in communist party leadership have severely hindered healthcare access for the general population. The allocation of healthcare resources, such as hospitals, medical equipment, and medication, is often influenced by personal connections rather than the needs of the public. This practice leads to a stark disparity in healthcare access between the privileged few and the marginalized majority. Diplomats need to recognize this inequality and advocate for fair and transparent distribution of healthcare resources.

Quality of Healthcare:

Corruption within healthcare systems under communist regimes directly impacts the quality of medical services provided. Nepotism often results in the appointment of underqualified individuals to key positions, compromising the expertise and competence of healthcare professionals. Additionally, corrupt practices such as bribery and embezzlement divert funds that should be allocated to improving healthcare infrastructure, staff training, and research. This ultimately undermines the quality of care available to the population. Diplomats must encourage the implementation of strict anti-corruption measures and support initiatives that promote professional development in the healthcare sector.

Public Health Systems:

Nepotism and corruption in public health systems pose significant threats to the well-being of individuals living under communist regimes. When healthcare decisions are influenced by personal connections rather than evidence-based practices, the focus shifts away from preventive measures and public health initiatives. This results in inadequate disease surveillance, vaccination programs, and health education campaigns. Diplomats should emphasize the importance of investing in public health infrastructure and policies to prevent the outbreak and spread of diseases.

Conclusion:

Nepotism and corruption in healthcare access and quality severely impact the lives of individuals living under communist regimes. Diplomats must address these issues and work towards implementing transparent and accountable healthcare systems. By advocating for fair distribution of resources, improving the competence of healthcare professionals, and prioritizing public health initiatives, diplomats can contribute to the improvement of healthcare access and quality in communist countries.

Case Studies: Prominent Examples of Nepotism and Corruption in Healthcare

Introduction:

In the realm of communist party leadership, nepotism and corruption have plagued various sectors, including healthcare and public health systems. This subchapter aims to shed light on some prominent examples of nepotism and corruption within the healthcare sector in communist regimes. By examining these case studies, diplomats and individuals interested in the topic will gain a deeper understanding of the challenges posed by nepotism and corruption in healthcare and public health systems.

Case Study 1: The Influence of Political Connections on Healthcare Access

In Country X, an influential communist party leader's family had direct control over the healthcare system. This resulted in preferential treatment for their family members and close associates, while the general population was neglected. Doctors and healthcare professionals who spoke out against this corruption were often silenced or faced severe consequences. This case study highlights the detrimental effects of nepotism on healthcare access for the general public.

Case Study 2: Misappropriation of Healthcare Funds

In Country Y, a corrupt communist party official siphoned off funds allocated for public health initiatives. These funds were meant to improve healthcare infrastructure, provide essential medical equipment, and enhance the quality of healthcare services. However, the official redirected these funds for personal gain, leaving the healthcare system severely under-resourced. This case study emphasizes the damaging impact of corruption on the overall healthcare system and the well-being of citizens.

Case Study 3: Sale of Counterfeit Medications

Country Z witnessed a widespread corruption scandal involving the sale of counterfeit medications within its healthcare system. Communist party officials colluded with pharmaceutical companies to distribute fake or substandard drugs, compromising the health and safety of patients. This case study underscores the risks associated with corruption in healthcare, where innocent lives are put at stake for personal gain.

Conclusion:

Nepotism and corruption in healthcare and public health systems within communist regimes have far-reaching consequences. The case studies presented here demonstrate the detrimental effects on healthcare access, misappropriation of funds, and the sale of counterfeit medications. As diplomats and individuals interested in combating corruption, it is crucial to recognize these issues and work towards implementing transparent and accountable systems within healthcare and public health sectors in communist countries. By doing so, we can strive towards a fair and equitable healthcare system that prioritizes the well-being of all citizens.

Chapter 7: Nepotism and Corruption in the Military and Defense Industries of Communist Countries

The Centralization of Power and Influence in Military Institutions

Title: The Centralization of Power and Influence in Military Institutions

Introduction:

In the intricate web of corruption and nepotism that weaves through communist party leadership, there lies a crucial subchapter that demands our undivided attention – "The Centralization of Power and Influence in Military Institutions." This chapter aims to shed light on the alarming levels of corruption and nepotism that taint the military and defense industries of communist countries. As diplomats and individuals invested in various niches affected by communist regimes, it is imperative that we understand the profound implications of this centralization of power and influence.

Paragraph 1:

The military and defense industries in communist countries often become breeding grounds for nepotism and corruption due to the significant influence they wield in shaping national security policies. Communist party leaders frequently exploit their positions to appoint family members, loyalists, and individuals with vested interests to key military roles. This practice not only compromises the meritocratic principles of military recruitment but also undermines the overall effectiveness and readiness of defense forces.

Paragraph 2:

The centralization of power and influence in military institutions further perpetuates corruption through illicit practices such as embezzlement, kickbacks, and bribery. State-owned defense enterprises, closely tied to the military, become hotbeds for embezzlement and misappropriation of funds. This siphoning of resources not only weakens the nation's defense capabilities but also deprives citizens of much-needed investments in critical areas like healthcare, education, and infrastructure.

Paragraph 3:

Moreover, the concentration of power within the military often extends beyond its immediate sphere and infiltrates other sectors. The military's influence on the media and propaganda machinery of communist regimes enables the dissemination of biased information, serving the interests of the ruling party. This manipulation of public opinion further perpetuates the centralization of power and suppresses dissenting voices, exacerbating the nepotism and corruption endemic in communist rule.

Paragraph 4:

Addressing the centralization of power and influence in military institutions requires a multi-faceted approach. Transparency, accountability, and meritocracy must be reinstated in military appointments and promotions. Robust oversight mechanisms, independent from the ruling party, should be established to combat corruption and ensure that resources are allocated appropriately. International cooperation and diplomatic pressure can play a pivotal role in encouraging communist countries to embrace democratic principles and enact meaningful reforms.

Conclusion:

As diplomats navigating the intricate world of nepotism and corruption within communist party leadership, it is crucial that we recognize the destructive consequences of the centralization of power and influence in military institutions. By shedding light on this issue, raising awareness, and advocating for necessary reforms, we can contribute to the dismantling of the deeply entrenched corruption that plagues communist regimes. Only through collective efforts can we strive for a future where meritocracy, transparency, and accountability prevail over nepotism and corruption, ensuring a just and prosperous society for all.

The Consequences of Nepotism and Corruption in Defense Sectors

Introduction:

The defense sector is a crucial aspect of any nation's stability and security. However, when nepotism and corruption infiltrate this domain, the consequences can be dire. This subchapter will delve into the various ramifications of nepotism and corruption in defense sectors, particularly in communist countries. Addressed to diplomats, this section will shed light on how these unethical practices affect not only the defense industries but also international relations.

Impact on Defense Capabilities:

Nepotism and corruption within defense sectors can severely undermine a country's defense capabilities. When positions of power are filled based on personal connections rather than merit, individuals lacking the necessary expertise may occupy key roles. This compromises the effectiveness of defense strategies and the development of advanced technologies. Consequently, the nation becomes vulnerable to external threats, endangering both national security and diplomatic relations.

Compromised National Security:

Nepotism and corruption often lead to compromised national security. Personal interests supersede the welfare of the state, as individuals in influential positions exploit their authority for personal gain. This can result in the leakage of sensitive information, compromised intelligence operations, and weakened defense mechanisms. Diplomats must be aware of these risks, as they can have far-reaching implications for international relations and regional stability.

Undermined Trust and Credibility:

When nepotism and corruption permeate defense sectors, trust and credibility are eroded both domestically and internationally. The public loses faith in the system, as they witness privileged individuals gaining access to positions without merit. This lack of transparency undermines the legitimacy of defense institutions, making it challenging for diplomats to build trust with these countries. Additionally, international partners become hesitant to collaborate, fearing that their own interests may be jeopardized by corrupt practices.

Economic Consequences:

Nepotism and corruption in defense sectors have significant economic implications. Financial resources that should be allocated for defense procurement and research are often misappropriated. This not only weakens the defense industries but also diverts funds from sectors crucial for economic development. Diplomats must recognize that economic stability and defense capabilities go hand in hand; corruption in defense sectors can have ripple effects on the overall economy, hindering investment and growth.

Conclusion:

Nepotism and corruption in defense sectors of communist countries have far-reaching consequences. The compromised defense capabilities, jeopardized national security, undermined trust and credibility, and economic repercussions all pose significant challenges for diplomats. To foster robust international relations, it is imperative to address and combat these unethical practices. By raising awareness, promoting transparency, and encouraging merit-based appointments, diplomats can work towards a more secure and trustworthy global defense landscape.

Case Studies: Notable Instances of Nepotism and Corruption in the Military

Introduction:

In this subchapter, we will delve into the dark underbelly of nepotism and corruption within the military and defense industries of communist countries. As diplomats, you are acutely aware of the importance of a strong and unbiased military force for national security. However, behind closed doors, nepotism and corruption have plagued these institutions, compromising their integrity and effectiveness. Through notable case studies, we will shed light on the extent of this issue and its implications.

Case Study 1: The Red Star Scandal

In the late 1980s, a major corruption scandal rocked the military of a prominent communist state. Known as the "Red Star Scandal," it exposed a network of high-ranking officers and their families who were involved in illegal arms sales, embezzlement, and kickbacks. This widespread corruption not only undermined the military's ability to defend the nation but also eroded public trust in the communist party's leadership.

Case Study 2: The Generals' Dynasty

In another communist country, a powerful military family dynasty emerged, leveraging their influence to secure high-ranking positions for their relatives. This nepotistic practice resulted in the appointment of inexperienced officers and compromised the meritocracy within the military hierarchy. As a consequence, morale plummeted, and the military's effectiveness was severely compromised, endangering national security.

Case Study 3: Defense Contracts and Kickbacks

The military-industrial complex in communist countries has often been a hotbed of corruption. In one striking case, defense contracts were awarded to companies owned by well-connected individuals, regardless of their competency. In return, these individuals would provide kickbacks to the military officials involved, diverting resources that should have been allocated for defense purposes. This corruption not only weakened the country's defense capabilities but also hindered technological advancements.

Implications and Way Forward:

Nepotism and corruption within the military and defense industries of communist countries have far-reaching consequences. They jeopardize national security, compromise the meritocratic principles necessary for a strong military, and undermine public confidence in the communist party's leadership. To address these issues, comprehensive reforms are needed, including transparent procurement processes, merit-based promotions, and strict penalties for corrupt practices. International cooperation and pressure can also play a vital role in encouraging change and ensuring accountability.

Conclusion:

The case studies presented herein provide a glimpse into the pervasive nepotism and corruption within the military and defense industries of communist countries. As diplomats, it is crucial to be aware of these challenges to effectively engage with communist regimes. By understanding the root causes and implications of nepotism and corruption, we can work towards fostering transparency, accountability, and meritocracy in military institutions worldwide, ultimately strengthening national security and promoting peace.

Chapter 8: Nepotism and Corruption in the Media and Propaganda Machinery of Communist Regimes

State Control and Censorship in Communist Media Systems

Introduction:

In the realm of communist countries, state control and censorship play a significant role in shaping the media landscape. This subchapter aims to shed light on the intricacies of state control and censorship within communist media systems, exposing the nepotism and corruption that often permeate these structures. By examining the control mechanisms employed by communist regimes, this subchapter seeks to provide diplomats with a comprehensive understanding of the challenges faced in the realm of media and propaganda machinery.

State Control and Censorship:

Communist regimes exercise tight control over media outlets, ensuring that the information disseminated aligns with the ruling party's ideologies and interests. In these systems, the state acts as the gatekeeper, determining what content is suitable for public consumption and suppressing any dissenting opinions. As a result, media outlets become tools for propaganda, serving the interests of the ruling elite rather than providing objective news coverage.

Nepotism and Corruption:

Nepotism and corruption are prevalent in communist media systems, with party loyalists often occupying key positions of power within these institutions. This allows the ruling party to control the narrative further and perpetuate its influence. Those favored by the party benefit from their positions, utilizing their power to suppress dissent and manipulate public opinion. The lack of transparency in the appointment process contributes to a culture of corruption, where personal connections and loyalty take precedence over merit and qualifications.

Censorship and Suppression of Dissent:

Censorship is a fundamental tool employed by communist regimes to maintain control over information flow. Critical voices, independent journalism, and alternative viewpoints are stifled, ensuring that only the party-approved narrative is disseminated. Journalists who dare to challenge the status quo face severe consequences, including harassment, imprisonment, or even violence. This suppression of dissent prevents the public from accessing diverse perspectives and fosters a climate of fear and self-censorship.

Conclusion:

State control and censorship in communist media systems are integral components of maintaining the ruling party's power and suppressing dissent. The nepotism and corruption that exist within these systems further exacerbate the manipulation of information and the stifling of independent journalism. By understanding the challenges faced in the realm of media and propaganda machinery, diplomats can work towards promoting freedom of the press, supporting independent voices, and advocating for transparency and accountability within communist regimes.

The Manipulation of Information through Nepotism and Corruption

Introduction:

In the realm of communist party leadership, nepotism and corruption have long been prevalent, resulting in the manipulation of information and a distortion of reality. This subchapter delves into the insidious nature of nepotism and corruption, examining their impact on various sectors crucial to the functioning of communist regimes. From state-owned enterprises and the judiciary to education and healthcare, this content aims to shed light on the detrimental effects of these practices. Addressed to diplomats, this chapter offers a comprehensive analysis of the far-reaching consequences of nepotism and corruption in communist party leadership.

Nepotism and Corruption in State-Owned Enterprises:

State-owned enterprises, essential components of communist economies, often fall prey to nepotism and corruption. Party leaders exploit their positions to place family members and loyal supporters in key roles, compromising the integrity and efficiency of these enterprises. This subchapter examines case studies, revealing how nepotism and corruption hinder innovation, breed inefficiency, and hinder economic growth.

Nepotism and Corruption in the Judiciary and Legal System:

The judiciary and legal system in communist countries are not immune to the toxic influence of nepotism and corruption. This section uncovers how judges, prosecutors, and lawyers are often appointed based on political loyalty rather than merit. Consequently, the impartiality and fairness of the legal system are compromised, leading to an erosion of trust and a disregard for the rule of law.

Nepotism and Corruption in Education and Healthcare:

Under communist rule, education and healthcare systems are expected to serve the collective good. However, nepotism and corruption infiltrate these sectors, undermining their primary objectives. This chapter investigates how nepotism affects access to quality education and healthcare, perpetuating inequality and hindering social mobility.

Nepotism and Corruption in the Military and Defense Industries:

The military and defense industries, integral to the survival and power of communist regimes, are particularly susceptible to nepotism and corruption. This section uncovers the consequences of placing unqualified individuals in positions of authority, compromising national security and defense capabilities.

Nepotism and Corruption in the Media and Propaganda Machinery:

Communist regimes heavily rely on the media and propaganda machinery to control information and shape public opinion. This subchapter explores how nepotism and corruption within these sectors distort reality, suppress dissent, and manipulate public perception to maintain the party's grip on power.

Nepotism and Corruption in Agricultural and Food Production Sectors:

Communist regimes often prioritize self-sufficiency in agricultural and food production. However, nepotism and corruption hinder efficiency, resulting in food shortages, malnutrition, and economic decline. This chapter examines the consequences of nepotism and corruption in these crucial sectors.

Nepotism and Corruption in Housing and Urban Development:

Communist regimes exert control over housing and urban development, often utilizing these sectors as tools of social control. This section explores how nepotism and corruption lead to inadequate housing, unequal distribution of resources, and the displacement of vulnerable communities.

Nepotism and Corruption in Foreign Aid and International Relations:

Communist countries engage in foreign aid and international relations to expand their influence and garner support. However, nepotism and corruption taint these endeavors, undermining trust, and diverting resources meant for development projects to personal gain. This chapter investigates the consequences of such practices on diplomatic relations and the credibility of communist regimes.

Conclusion:

Nepotism and corruption within communist party leadership have far-reaching consequences across sectors critical to the functioning of these regimes. This subchapter reveals the manipulation of information, distortion of reality, and erosion of trust resulting from these practices. By shedding light on these issues, diplomats and those interested in the niches of nepotism and corruption in communist party leadership gain a comprehensive understanding of the challenges faced by these regimes and the urgent need for reform.

Case Studies: Infamous Examples of Nepotism and Corruption in the Media

In the world of communist party leadership, nepotism and corruption extend their tentacles into every aspect of society, including the media and propaganda machinery. This subchapter explores some infamous case studies that shed light on the extent of nepotism and corruption within this sphere.

One such example comes from the state-controlled media in a communist regime, where family ties often determine who gets the opportunity to influence public opinion. In this case, a high-ranking party official appointed his own son as the editor-in-chief of a prominent newspaper. This nepotistic appointment compromised the newspaper's independence, as the editor-in-chief used his position to advance his father's political agenda and silence dissenting voices.

Another case study highlights the collusion between the media and the judiciary in a communist country. In this instance, a judge with close ties to the ruling party utilized his influence to secure favorable coverage from a state-owned television channel. By providing exclusive interviews and access to court proceedings, the judge ensured that he received favorable treatment in the media, shielding him from scrutiny and allowing him to continue engaging in corrupt practices.

The media's role in disseminating propaganda is also ripe for corruption. In one particularly egregious example, a state-run television station in a communist country fabricated stories to manipulate public opinion and suppress dissent. Journalists who attempted to report the truth were fired or faced violence and intimidation. This case study serves as a stark reminder of the dangers posed by a media apparatus controlled by nepotistic and corrupt individuals.

Ultimately, these case studies expose the insidious nature of nepotism and corruption in the media and propaganda machinery of communist regimes. The manipulation of information not only undermines the integrity of journalism but also perpetuates an environment of repression and censorship. Diplomats and those interested in the various niches of communist party leadership must be aware of these examples to better understand the challenges posed by nepotism and corruption within the media sector, as well as its wider implications for other sectors, such as foreign aid and international relations.

By shining a light on these infamous case studies, this subchapter aims to provoke discussions and encourage diplomatic efforts towards combating nepotism and corruption in the media, ultimately contributing to the development of more transparent and accountable communist party leadership.

Chapter 9: Nepotism and Corruption in the Agricultural and Food Production Sectors under Communist Rule

State Ownership and Collective Farming in Communist Agricultural Systems

In the intricate web of nepotism and corruption that plagues communist party leadership, one must not overlook the significant role played by state ownership and collective farming in the agricultural sector. The state's control over land and food production has been a double-edged sword, providing ample opportunities for exploitation and abuse of power.

Under communist regimes, the agricultural sector is often centralized and administered by the state, with private ownership of land virtually non-existent. This concentration of power, coupled with the absence of market mechanisms, creates an environment ripe for corruption and nepotism. Party leaders, their relatives, and loyalists often exploit their positions to amass wealth, acquire valuable land, and control the distribution of resources.

Collective farming, a cornerstone of communist agricultural systems, further exacerbates the problem. In theory, it is meant to promote equality and communal cooperation. However, in reality, it often leads to inefficiency, poor management, and the concentration of power in the hands of a few. The lack of individual incentives, combined with the absence of competition, allows nepotism to flourish, as influential party members allocate resources and privileges to their kin, while neglecting the needs of the wider community.

In addition, the absence of transparent and accountable institutions in communist agricultural systems provides a breeding ground for corruption. Party-appointed officials, often lacking the necessary expertise, frequently abuse their positions for personal gain. They may demand bribes for favorable treatment, manipulate the allocation of subsidies, or divert resources meant for the agricultural sector into their own pockets.

The consequences of this nepotism and corruption in communist agricultural systems are dire. Inefficient resource allocation, low productivity, and food shortages become the norm. The lack of investment and innovation stifles agricultural development, leading to declining living standards, malnutrition, and even famine. The effects are felt not only by the rural population but also by urban dwellers who depend on a stable food supply.

To address these issues, it is crucial for diplomats and international actors to recognize the systemic flaws inherent in communist agricultural systems. Support for transparent governance, the rule of law, and market-oriented reforms can help foster a more accountable and efficient agricultural sector. By empowering farmers, encouraging private ownership of land, and promoting fair competition, the potential for corruption and nepotism can be mitigated, leading to a more sustainable and equitable food production system.

In conclusion, state ownership and collective farming in communist agricultural systems have provided fertile ground for nepotism and corruption. The concentration of power, lack of competition, and absence of accountable institutions have allowed party leaders and their relatives to exploit their positions at the expense of the wider population. Recognizing these issues and supporting reforms that promote transparency and market mechanisms can pave the way for a more prosperous and equitable agricultural sector.

The Impact of Nepotism and Corruption on Food Security and Efficiency

Introduction:

In this subchapter, we will delve into the profound impact that nepotism and corruption have on food security and efficiency within communist regimes. By focusing on the agricultural and food production sectors under communist rule, we aim to shed light on the detrimental consequences of these practices. This chapter is addressed to diplomats and individuals interested in the niche areas of nepotism and corruption in communist party leadership, state-owned enterprises, judiciary, education, healthcare, military, media, housing, urban development, foreign aid, and international relations of communist countries.

1. The Agricultural and Food Production Sectors:

Nepotism and corruption in agricultural and food production sectors have severe implications for food security and efficiency. By favoring family members or allies for key positions, qualified individuals are often bypassed, leading to incompetence and mismanagement. This incompetence can result in reduced productivity, substandard quality of agricultural products, and inefficient distribution systems, all of which ultimately compromise food security.

2. Misallocation of Resources:

Corruption within communist regimes often leads to the misallocation of resources in the agricultural sector. Funds that should be invested in infrastructure development, modern technology, and agricultural research are diverted for personal gain. This misallocation hinders the sector's ability to enhance productivity and meet the rising food demands of the population, exacerbating food security concerns.

3. Lack of Accountability and Transparency:

Nepotism and corruption undermine accountability and transparency within the agricultural and food production sectors. In the absence of a merit-based system, officials are less likely to be held accountable for their actions, leading to a culture of impunity. This lack of transparency further perpetuates corrupt practices and prevents the implementation of effective policies to ensure food security and efficiency.

4. Impacts on Farmers and Consumers:

Farmers, who are at the forefront of food production, suffer the most under nepotism and corruption. Limited access to resources, unfair pricing systems, and lack of government support hinder their ability to increase productivity and improve their livelihoods. Additionally, consumers face the consequences of inefficiencies within the system, with higher prices, lower quality products, and limited access to nutritious food.

Conclusion:

Nepotism and corruption within communist regimes have far-reaching consequences on food security and efficiency in the agricultural and food production sectors. By favoring personal interests over the welfare of the population, these practices hinder the development of sustainable and productive agricultural systems. It is imperative for diplomats and individuals interested in these niche areas to address these challenges and advocate for transparent and accountable governance to ensure food security for all.

Case Studies: Noteworthy Instances of Nepotism and Corruption in Agriculture

Title: Case Studies: Noteworthy Instances of Nepotism and Corruption in Agriculture

Introduction:

Welcome to the subchapter on "Case Studies: Noteworthy Instances of Nepotism and Corruption in Agriculture." In this section, we will delve into the dark underbelly of nepotism and corruption that have plagued the agricultural and food production sectors under communist rule. Through a series of carefully selected case studies, we aim to shed light on the detrimental impact these practices have had on these vital industries.

Case Study 1: The Great Famine of China (1959-1961):

One of the most infamous instances of nepotism and corruption in agriculture occurred during the Great Famine in China. The communist regime's misguided policies and promotion of unqualified individuals within the agricultural sector resulted in a catastrophic event that claimed the lives of millions. Nepotism and corruption hindered the implementation of effective agricultural practices, exacerbating the food shortages and leading to widespread famine.

Case Study 2: Collective Farms in the Soviet Union:

The Soviet Union's collectivization policy aimed to consolidate agriculture into large state-run farms. However, nepotism and corruption within these collectives allowed party officials and their relatives to seize control over prime agricultural land and resources. This led to inefficiencies, reduced productivity, and ultimately contributed to food shortages and economic decline.

Case Study 3: Land Redistribution in North Korea:

In North Korea, the government's land redistribution policies were marred by nepotism and corruption. Land was often allocated based on political loyalty rather than agricultural expertise, resulting in inexperienced individuals taking charge of farming operations. This mismanagement led to decreased agricultural output, exacerbating food insecurity in the country.

Case Study 4: Agriculture and Cronyism in Cuba:

Cuba's agricultural sector has long been plagued by nepotism and corruption. The Communist Party's control over land allocation, subsidies, and markets favored party loyalists and their families, stifling competition and innovation. As a result, the agricultural sector in Cuba has struggled to meet the population's food demands, leading to heavy reliance on imports.

Conclusion:

These case studies highlight the detrimental effects of nepotism and corruption in the agricultural and food production sectors under communist rule. The lack of merit-based appointments, favoritism, and mismanagement have resulted in widespread food shortages, economic decline, and increased dependence on foreign aid. As diplomats and individuals concerned with these issues, it is crucial to address and combat these practices to ensure the well-being and prosperity of agricultural communities in communist countries.

Chapter 10: Nepotism and Corruption in the Housing and Urban Development Sectors in Communist Regimes

State Control and Allocation of Housing in Communist Societies

Introduction:

In the realm of communist societies, the state's control and allocation of housing have been an integral part of the overall system. This subchapter aims to shed light on the various aspects of this control and allocation, unveiling the nepotism and corruption that often accompany it. By examining the housing and urban development sectors under communist rule, diplomats and individuals interested in the intricacies of nepotism and corruption will gain valuable insights into this crucial aspect of communist party leadership.

Summary of Content:

1. The Role of State in Housing Allocation:

In communist societies, the state assumes a dominant role in the allocation of housing. This enables the government to exert control over the distribution of housing resources, leading to potential opportunities for nepotism and corruption within the process.

2. Nepotism in Housing Allocation:

Communist party leaders often abuse their authority and privilege to allocate housing to their own family members or close associates. This nepotistic practice undermines the principles of equality and fairness that are often touted by communist regimes.

3. Corruption in Housing Development Projects:

The housing and urban development sectors in communist societies are susceptible to corruption. Party leaders and government officials may engage in bribery, embezzlement, or favoritism to secure lucrative contracts for construction projects, leading to subpar housing quality and misallocation of resources.

4. Discrimination in Housing Allocation:

Housing allocation in communist societies is not always based on merit, but rather on loyalty to the party or personal connections. This discriminatory practice excludes individuals who may be more deserving of housing, perpetuating social inequality.

5. Lack of Transparency and Accountability:

Communist regimes often lack transparency and accountability in the housing sector. The absence of checks and balances allows for unchecked nepotism and corruption to thrive, further eroding public trust in the government.

Conclusion:

The state control and allocation of housing in communist societies have provided fertile ground for nepotism and corruption. By understanding the extent of these issues, diplomats can gain a comprehensive understanding of the challenges faced by communist party leadership. Furthermore, it is crucial to recognize the detrimental effects of nepotism and corruption on housing quality, social equality, and public trust. Addressing these issues is vital for the development of fair and transparent housing policies within communist societies.

The Influence of Nepotism and Corruption on Urban Development

Introduction:

Nepotism and corruption have long been pervasive issues in communist party leadership, affecting various sectors of society. This subchapter delves into the impact of nepotism and corruption specifically on urban development. By exploring this topic, diplomats, along with individuals interested in the niches of nepotism and corruption in communist party leadership, can gain a deeper understanding of the detrimental effects these practices have on the development of urban areas.

Nepotism and Corruption in Urban Development:

Urban development plays a crucial role in fostering economic growth, improving living standards, and creating sustainable communities. However, when nepotism and corruption infiltrate the process, the outcomes are often compromised. Communist regimes have witnessed the negative consequences of nepotism and corruption in the housing and urban development sectors.

Nepotism in Urban Planning:

One of the key ways nepotism impacts urban development is through biased decision-making in urban planning. Communist party leaders often prioritize their own interests or those of their close associates, leading to the neglect of public welfare. This results in inadequate infrastructure, substandard housing, and inadequate public services, ultimately hindering the progress of urban areas.

Corruption in Construction Projects:

Corruption further exacerbates the problems associated with urban development. In communist regimes, construction projects are notorious for being arenas of corruption. Bribes, kickbacks, and embezzlement become common practices, leading to the use of substandard materials, cost overruns, and delays in project completion. As a result, urban areas suffer from poorly constructed buildings, unsafe infrastructure, and a lack of essential amenities.

Social and Economic Consequences:

The influence of nepotism and corruption on urban development extends beyond physical structures. These practices also have profound social and economic consequences. The unequal distribution of resources and opportunities creates a divided society, where the rich get richer and the poor struggle to improve their living conditions. Moreover, corruption hampers investment and economic growth, deterring foreign aid and exacerbating poverty in urban areas.

Conclusion:

The detrimental influence of nepotism and corruption on urban development in communist countries cannot be understated. Diplomats and individuals interested in this topic must recognize the urgent need for reforms to combat these practices. By addressing nepotism and corruption, communist party leaders can foster inclusive and sustainable urban development, leading to prosperous communities and improved living standards for all.

Case Studies: Prominent Examples of Nepotism and Corruption in Housing and Urban Development

Introduction:

In the realm of communist party leadership, corruption and nepotism have been pervasive issues that have plagued various sectors, including housing and urban development. This subchapter aims to shed light on some prominent case studies that showcase the extent of these problems within this specific sector.

Case Study 1: The Great Housing Scandal in Country X

Country X, a communist regime, witnessed a massive corruption scandal in its housing and urban development sector. High-ranking party officials and their family members were found to have abused their power, engaging in nepotism and embezzlement of funds meant for public housing projects. The scandal resulted in an acute shortage of affordable housing for the general population, while the elite few enjoyed luxurious accommodations.

Case Study 2: Cronyism and Graft in City Y's Urban Development

City Y, under communist party rule, experienced an alarming case of nepotism and corruption in its urban development sector. Local party leaders collaborated with influential businessmen to exploit their positions for personal gain. This led to the misallocation of land and resources, favoring those with connections and leaving the urban poor marginalized. The city's infrastructure development suffered, and the quality of housing projects deteriorated, while the corrupt officials amassed significant wealth.

Case Study 3: Kickbacks and Bribes in Mega City Z's Housing Projects

Mega City Z, a major metropolis in a communist country, faced rampant corruption in its housing sector. Party officials abused their authority by soliciting kickbacks and bribes from real estate developers in exchange for preferential treatment in obtaining permits and licenses. This illicit practice severely compromised the quality of housing and urban development, as substandard materials were used, endangering the lives of residents. The disadvantaged were further marginalized as affordable housing initiatives were hijacked by corrupt officials and their associates.

Conclusion:

These case studies provide a glimpse into the alarming prevalence of nepotism and corruption within the housing and urban development sectors under communist party leadership. The consequences of these unethical practices include a scarcity of affordable housing, misallocation of resources, and compromised infrastructure. Diplomats and individuals interested in understanding the challenges faced by communist countries in these sectors should consider these case studies as compelling evidence of the urgent need for transparency and accountability in order to address the systemic issues of nepotism and corruption.

Chapter 11: Nepotism and Corruption in Foreign Aid and International Relations of Communist Countries

The Use of Foreign Aid as a Tool for Nepotism and Corruption

Introduction:

In the complex web of nepotism and corruption that plagues communist party leadership, one often overlooked aspect is the role of foreign aid. While foreign aid is intended to provide assistance and support to developing countries, it can inadvertently become a tool for furthering nepotism and corruption within the recipient nation. This subchapter delves into the dark underbelly of foreign aid in the context of communist regimes, shedding light on how these funds are manipulated to serve the interests of the ruling elite.

Foreign Aid as a Facilitator of Nepotism:

Foreign aid, when funneled through communist party leadership, allows for blatant nepotism to thrive. The ruling elite, often comprised of party officials and their families, manipulate the allocation of aid funds to benefit themselves and their cronies. This not only perpetuates a culture of favoritism but also undermines meritocracy and hinders the development of a fair and equal society.

Corruption in the Distribution of Foreign Aid:

Corruption is an inherent risk in the distribution of foreign aid, especially in communist regimes. The lack of transparency and accountability makes it easier for party officials to siphon off aid funds for personal gain. Whether through embezzlement, bribery, or kickbacks, corruption seeps into every level of the aid distribution process, diverting funds away from the intended beneficiaries and into the pockets of the corrupt few.

The Impact on Development Sectors:

The consequences of nepotism and corruption in the use of foreign aid are far-reaching. The education sector, healthcare system, and agricultural and food production sectors, among others, are severely affected. Limited resources are misallocated, leading to a decline in the quality of education, healthcare services, and food security. This perpetuates a cycle of poverty and inequality, exacerbating the very problems foreign aid aims to alleviate.

International Relations and Foreign Aid:

The misappropriation of foreign aid not only damages the domestic development of communist countries but also strains their international relations. Donor countries, often diplomatic partners, become disillusioned by the misuse of aid funds. This erodes trust and hinders future cooperation, further isolating communist regimes from the global community.

Conclusion:

Foreign aid, when exploited as a tool for nepotism and corruption, perpetuates a vicious cycle of inequality and undermines the development of communist countries. Diplomats and those interested in the various niches of nepotism and corruption in communist party leadership need to be aware of this insidious practice. By exposing and addressing these issues, we can work towards a more transparent and accountable system that ensures foreign aid is used for its intended purpose – uplifting the lives of the most vulnerable in society.

The Impact of Nepotism and Corruption on International Relations

Introduction:

Nepotism and corruption have long been intertwined in the fabric of communist party leadership. These unethical practices extend beyond political boundaries and have a profound impact on international relations. This subchapter aims to shed light on the consequences of nepotism and corruption in various sectors of communist regimes, highlighting their implications for diplomacy and global cooperation.

Nepotism and Corruption in Communist Party Leadership:

The communist party leadership often becomes a breeding ground for nepotism and corruption. The concentration of power in the hands of a few individuals allows for the manipulation of resources and favors, leading to a lack of transparency and accountability. This not only erodes the public's trust in the government but also hampers diplomatic relations with other nations.

Nepotism and Corruption in State-Owned Enterprises:

State-owned enterprises are particularly vulnerable to nepotism and corruption due to their close ties with the communist party leadership. Unfair procurement practices, embezzlement, and favoritism towards family members and close associates hinder healthy competition and discourage foreign investment. This not only damages the economic landscape but also strains international trade relations.

Nepotism and Corruption in the Judiciary and Legal System:

An impartial and trustworthy judiciary is essential for maintaining the rule of law and ensuring justice. However, nepotism and corruption in the judiciary undermine its credibility and impartiality. This further weakens the legal system, making it difficult for foreign investors to trust the fairness of legal proceedings and complicating international legal cooperation.

Nepotism and Corruption in Education and Healthcare:

Education and healthcare systems are vital for the development and well-being of a nation. However, under communist rule, nepotism and corruption often result in substandard education and healthcare services. This not only hampers human development but also affects international cooperation in these sectors, making it challenging to establish meaningful partnerships and exchange of knowledge.

Nepotism and Corruption in the Military and Defense Industries:

Nepotism and corruption in the military and defense industries compromise national security and hinder international collaboration. The allocation of defense contracts to family members and associates based on personal relationships rather than merit undermines the effectiveness of defense forces. Such practices also raise concerns among other nations regarding the transparency and reliability of military cooperation.

Nepotism and Corruption in Media and Propaganda:

Media and propaganda play a crucial role in shaping public opinion and maintaining transparency. However, under communist regimes, media outlets often become tools for disseminating biased information and suppressing dissent. This undermines the credibility of the media and complicates international communication, hindering diplomatic relations and cooperation.

Nepotism and Corruption in Agriculture, Housing, and Urban Development:

Nepotism and corruption in the agricultural and housing sectors result in unequal distribution of resources and poor urban planning. This not only affects the well-being of citizens but also poses challenges to international trade and cooperation in these sectors. Unfair practices and lack of transparency limit foreign investments, impeding sustainable development and global collaboration.

Nepotism and Corruption in Foreign Aid and International Relations:

Nepotism and corruption in the allocation of foreign aid and conduct of international relations harm diplomatic ties and hinder international cooperation. The diversion of funds meant for development projects and the prioritization of personal relationships over diplomatic principles undermine trust and credibility. This makes it difficult for communist countries to engage meaningfully with the international community and limits their ability to foster positive international relations.

Conclusion:

The impact of nepotism and corruption in communist party leadership extends far beyond national borders, tarnishing international relations in various sectors. To build trust and foster cooperation, it is imperative for communist regimes to address these issues, promote transparency, and establish accountable systems in all domains. Only then can meaningful diplomacy and international collaboration thrive, leading to a more just and prosperous global community.

Case Studies: Notable Instances of Nepotism and Corruption in Foreign Aid and International Relations

Introduction:

As diplomats, it is crucial to be aware of the pervasive nepotism and corruption that plague communist party leadership. This subchapter aims to shed light on the specific instances of nepotism and corruption in foreign aid and international relations within communist countries. By examining these case studies, we can garner a deeper understanding of the challenges and implications that arise from such practices.

Case Study 1: The Red Cross Scandal

In a prominent communist country, the Red Cross became a victim of nepotism and corruption within its international aid initiatives. Senior Party officials used their positions to direct aid towards their family members and allies, rather than those in genuine need. This scandal not only undermined the credibility of the Red Cross but also hindered the country's international relations.

Case Study 2: Exploitative Resource Extraction Agreements

In another communist regime, corrupt officials colluded with foreign corporations, granting them favorable resource extraction agreements in exchange for personal gain. This practice not only led to the exploitation of natural resources but also perpetuated a cycle of poverty and inequality within the country. Such corruption tarnished the nation's reputation and hindered its ability to establish equitable international relations.

Case Study 3: Influence Peddling in International Organizations

Communist party leaders have been known to wield their influence in international organizations to their advantage. By placing their relatives or close associates in key positions within these organizations, they ensure a favorable outcome for their country. However, this blatant nepotism compromises the integrity and fairness of these organizations, eroding trust and damaging international relations.

Case Study 4: Misappropriation of Foreign Aid Funds

Foreign aid, intended to uplift the lives of the underprivileged, has often fallen victim to corruption within communist regimes. Officials divert aid funds meant for healthcare, education, and infrastructure development, channeling them into personal bank accounts. This misappropriation not only deprives the intended beneficiaries but also strains diplomatic relations, as donor countries question the efficacy of their aid.

Conclusion:

The case studies presented here highlight the far-reaching consequences of nepotism and corruption in foreign aid and international relations within communist countries. By understanding and addressing these issues, diplomats can work towards fostering transparency, fairness, and accountability in international engagements. It is imperative that steps are taken to combat nepotism and corruption, as they undermine both the integrity of communist party leadership and the trust of the international community.

Chapter 12: Conclusion and Recommendations for Reform

The Need for Addressing Nepotism and Corruption in Communist Party Leadership

Introduction:

The Communist Party leadership plays a pivotal role in shaping the policies and governance of communist regimes. However, the issue of nepotism and corruption within this leadership has been a persistent problem, hampering the progress and development of these nations. This subchapter aims to shed light on the urgent need to address nepotism and corruption in the Communist Party leadership, exploring its detrimental effects on various sectors such as state-owned enterprises, the judiciary, education, healthcare, defense, media, agriculture, housing, and foreign aid.

Nepotism and Corruption in Communist Party Leadership:

Nepotism, the practice of favoring relatives or close associates in appointments and promotions, creates a breeding ground for corruption. This subchapter will delve into the detrimental consequences of nepotism and corruption within the Communist Party leadership and its impact on the overall governance of communist regimes.

State-Owned Enterprises:

Nepotism and corruption within state-owned enterprises under communist regimes result in inefficiency, economic stagnation, and unfair competition. This section will discuss specific cases and their adverse effects on the economy and the well-being of citizens.

Judiciary and Legal System:

A corrupt judiciary undermines the rule of law, erodes public trust, and hampers justice delivery. By examining case studies and examples, this subchapter will highlight how nepotism and corruption within the judiciary and legal system of communist countries have far-reaching implications for citizens' rights and the overall democratic fabric.

Education Sector:

Nepotism and corruption in the education sector under communist rule can compromise the quality of education, deny opportunities to deserving individuals, and perpetuate inequality. This section will explore the consequences and propose solutions to counter these issues.

Healthcare and Public Health Systems:

Corruption and nepotism within healthcare and public health systems in communist regimes can lead to inadequate access to medical services, compromised patient care, and the misallocation of resources. This subchapter will examine the impact of these practices on public health and suggest measures to address the challenges.

Conclusion:

Addressing nepotism and corruption in the Communist Party leadership is crucial for the sustainable development and progress of communist regimes. By examining the adverse effects of these practices on various sectors like state-owned enterprises, the judiciary, education, healthcare, defense, media, agriculture, housing, and foreign aid, this subchapter aims to raise awareness among diplomats and key stakeholders. It emphasizes the urgency to implement comprehensive reforms and establish transparent systems that foster accountability, meritocracy, and equal opportunities for all. Only by tackling nepotism and corruption can communist countries strive towards a more just, prosperous, and equitable future.

Potential Strategies for Combating Nepotism and Corruption in Communist Regimes

Introduction:

The prevalence of nepotism and corruption in communist party leadership, state-owned enterprises, judiciary, education, healthcare, military, media, agriculture, housing, and foreign aid sectors is a pressing concern in many communist regimes. This subchapter aims to provide potential strategies that can be employed to combat nepotism and corruption in these specific areas.

1. Strengthening Transparency and Accountability:

Implementing transparent systems and procedures in various sectors can help minimize opportunities for nepotism and corruption. This can include establishing independent oversight bodies, enhancing financial auditing processes, and promoting public access to information.

2. Merit-Based Recruitment and Promotion Practices:

Introducing merit-based recruitment and promotion practices can help ensure that qualified individuals are selected based on their skills, qualifications, and experience rather than familial or personal connections. Implementing standardized and transparent selection criteria can mitigate the influence of nepotism and corruption.

3. Robust Anti-Corruption Legislation and Enforcement:

Enacting comprehensive anti-corruption laws and regulations is vital for combating nepotism and corruption. These laws should include provisions for severe penalties and deterrents, as well as protection for whistleblowers. Furthermore, establishing specialized anti-corruption agencies with adequate resources and independence can enhance enforcement efforts.

4. Promoting Civic Education and Awareness:

Educating citizens about the detrimental effects of nepotism and corruption is crucial for building a culture of integrity. By promoting civic education programs and awareness campaigns, individuals will be empowered to demand accountability and actively participate in anti-corruption initiatives.

5. International Cooperation and Pressure:

Engaging in international cooperation can exert pressure on communist regimes to address nepotism and corruption. Diplomats can work collaboratively through multilateral organizations, such as the United Nations, to advocate for transparent governance and anti-corruption measures.

6. Strengthening Civil Society and Independent Media:

Supporting civil society organizations and independent media outlets can serve as watchdogs and expose instances of nepotism and corruption. Providing financial assistance, protection, and training to these entities can help ensure their effectiveness in holding authorities accountable.

7. Whistleblower Protection and Incentives:

Establishing robust whistleblower protection mechanisms and providing incentives for reporting corruption can encourage individuals to come forward with information. Protection from retaliation and rewards for exposing corruption can help uncover instances of nepotism and corruption in various sectors.

Conclusion:

Combating nepotism and corruption in communist regimes requires a multi-faceted approach. Strengthening transparency, enforcing anti-corruption laws, promoting civic education, fostering international cooperation, supporting civil society, and protecting whistleblowers are all critical strategies that can contribute to addressing these pervasive issues. By implementing these strategies, diplomats and stakeholders can work towards creating fairer and more accountable communist systems.

The Role of Diplomats in Promoting Transparency and Accountability in Communist Countries

In the ever-changing landscape of global politics, diplomats play a crucial role in promoting transparency and accountability in communist countries. This subchapter explores how diplomats can navigate the complex webs of nepotism and corruption that exist within the leadership of communist party regimes, state-owned enterprises, judiciary and legal systems, education sector, healthcare and public health systems, military and defense industries, media and propaganda machinery, agricultural and food production sectors, housing and urban development sectors, as well as foreign aid and international relations.

Diplomats, as representatives of their respective countries, have the unique opportunity to influence and shape the policies and practices of communist regimes. By engaging in diplomatic dialogues and negotiations, they can advocate for transparent governance structures that promote accountability and discourage nepotism and corruption. Open discussions with communist leaders can help foster a culture of transparency, where leaders are held accountable for their actions and decisions.

In the realm of state-owned enterprises, diplomats can promote transparency by advocating for the implementation of fair and competitive procurement processes. By encouraging the adoption of international standards and best practices, diplomats can ensure that state-owned enterprises operate with integrity, free from nepotism and corruption.

Similarly, within the judiciary and legal systems, diplomats can push for the independence of the judiciary and the establishment of an impartial legal framework. By supporting training programs for judges and lawyers, diplomats can help build a judiciary that upholds the principles of transparency and accountability.

In the education sector, diplomats can work towards fostering a merit-based system that values qualifications and competence over political connections. By supporting educational exchange programs and scholarships, diplomats can empower students to pursue knowledge and skills without the burden of nepotism and corruption.

Diplomats can also play a crucial role in promoting transparency and accountability in the healthcare and public health systems of communist regimes. By advocating for the allocation of resources towards healthcare infrastructure, diplomats can ensure that the needs of the population are met in a fair and equitable manner.

In the military and defense industries, diplomats can encourage the establishment of oversight mechanisms to prevent corruption and nepotism. By promoting transparency in defense procurement and sales, diplomats can help build trust and confidence in these crucial sectors.

Furthermore, diplomats can engage with the media and propaganda machinery to promote freedom of the press and encourage responsible journalism. By supporting initiatives that foster investigative reporting and protect journalists, diplomats can help expose corruption and nepotism in the public sphere.

In the agricultural and food production sectors, diplomats can advocate for reforms that empower small-scale farmers and promote sustainable practices. By supporting initiatives that increase transparency in land ownership and distribution, diplomats can help combat corruption and promote equitable development.

Finally, in the realm of foreign aid and international relations, diplomats can promote transparency and accountability by ensuring that aid is distributed in a fair and efficient manner. By working with international organizations and civil society groups, diplomats can help monitor the use of aid funds and ensure that they are not misappropriated for personal gain.

In conclusion, diplomats have a crucial role to play in promoting transparency and accountability in communist countries. By engaging in diplomatic dialogues, advocating for reforms, and supporting initiatives that foster transparency, diplomats can contribute to the creation of more accountable and transparent governance structures in communist regimes.